TIM HERZBERG

AF171098

HALE
TIME
EXPERIENCES OF A NEURO

for the veggies

Text and Layout

Tim Herzberg

Title image

Image taken in the computer tomograph of the University Clinic Eppendorf on October 11, 2009

Publisher

BoD – Books on Demand

ISBN

9783732287000

1st Edition

© 2013 Tim Herzberg

More on half-time.info

1. A nightmare

In advance, to all the things that happened to me in this book, I'm doing fine. But I did have a stroke (pun intended!) of bad luck. I woke up in the morning on the eleventh of October 2009, with no feeling or movement in my left side, and it wasn't even much of a surprise. Don't get me wrong, it was definitely a real surprise that it was happening to me. No questions whatsoever. It's just that I'd had no headaches, no high blood pressure; I didn't smoke too much. Not too much alcohol, the occasional glass of wine or two on the balcony with my wife. At parties more, but you see, we all get older and being in the middle of my thirties, the time of delirium parties had pretty much gone by. The part that wasn't surprising was that I knew pretty fast what had happened. I had seen a report on strokes with young people on TV the night before. The symptoms were easy enough to identify and the implications were clear: something had gone terribly wrong with the right side of my brain. Most likely a stroke, highly improbable, but it wasn't out of the question. It was just the same with the bloke on TV. Weird enough I had just read about the new stroke unit in the University clinic in Eppendorf (UKE). I rang up Jessica, a good friend of mine. Her Husbands a bit bigger. He was an American Footballer, defence line, and most importantly, she had a key to the flat. I just barely made it to my mobile. They came, helped me into clothes and carried me the three floors down. They then called a cab and came with me to the UKE. According to her, it was the slowest cabride of all time. An ambulance would have taken me to a closer but wrong hospital (no stroke unit). My blackout starts at the casualty entrance. So most of the coming events are only hearsay.

2. Dead of night

My wife was at the airport in Frankfurt well on her way to a workshop on the Philippines, or Singapore as the phone call hit her. She took the first flight back to Hamburg. Allegedly a nurse explained to me that my head needed to be scanned.

"No shit, Sherlock,", "but not with X-ray or CT (computer tomography)."

"We've got something newer and better…" She said. I just thought:

"Ok, so the UKE has already got a magnetic resonance imager (MRI)". She went on:

" …it's a big round box that looks bit like an oversized washing machine and it makes scary noises".

She probably thought I had already been sedated or something, so I explained it to her. In detail. I started with Basics: Atomic spin, moving along quickly to the law of conservation of angular momentum and how you can use it on atomic nuclei and rotating electron probability clouds, which I explained in depth. For some reason she gave up quickly.

So I was scanned. Let's take a look first. This scan is depicted on the front of the book. What they found was major brain haemorrhage (the large white area), a huge intra cerebral bleeding (ICB), a large amount of blood leaking into my brain. The reason was unknown.

Whilst scanning a second bleeding put so much pressure on more important parts of my brain that I stopped breathing and lost consciousness. I was artificially ventilated first with a bag valve mask resuscitator (the footy thing with the gasmask). Later I was intubed.

Ok, patient stable, what next? A couple of minutes later I was in an operating room still unconscious, with a drill well on its way into my skull, doing quite well, having my first go at brain surgery. And it was not to be my last.

They let off the dangerous high pressure. The brain surgeons hoped that my respiratory system would come back. They were right. "Nurse, would you comb his hair back over the hole. Ok, yes, it is a rather big hole. Look, I can stick a finger in his brain cavity. Ok, then forget the comb, sew him up. After that, we'll send him into deep space. Let's use opiates today; he's got lots more coming at him."

About a week later I had to shake hands with a brain surgeon to see if I'm not a vegetable yet and to check if going on makes sense at all. I wasn't a veggie, and on it went.

Later they told me that I wouldn't have survived the second bleed in the back of an ambulance. It was just unbelievable luck that they were "watching" at that very moment and were able to react quickly. It was a matter of not minutes but more of seconds. Had I, back in bed, thought "it'll probably go away", just like when you lie on your arm while sleeping and it wakes up numb with that pins and needles feeling. I'd be dead now had I misjudged the symptoms. I had a close shave with death and survived with a lot of luck on my side. And I still wasn't in a position to bargain, yet.

By this time they had put a hole in my windpipe, a classic tracheotomy tube. This is a tube that goes through the frontal base of your neck all the way into your windpipe and down it a good ten centimetres. This has one advantage, it goes past annoying bits of anatomy like your nose or your tongue that can get in the way and disturb your breathing. I needed assistance and a higher oxygen level and because no one could sit there all day and pump air into my lungs I was plugged into life sustaining machines. Now that's spooky.

In the meantime they had found out what had happened. The reason for my ICB was an AVM. Ok, I got it, explanation first then abbreviation. It was a prenatally (before birth, where everything is still soft and malleable formed Arteriovenous malformation (AVM). And it was so small it was hard to detect without specifically knowing what to look for beforehand.

I had been going about my life without knowing that I had a time bomb ticking away in my head. Ok, ok, explanation: these malformations are created when an artery (high pressure system) gets too close to a vein (low pressure system). As a result of pressure compensation a capillary meshwork is produced. This can't stand up to high pressure. It just blows at some time or another.

This happens often, but when it happens in your finger or calf you just get a bruise. When it happens in your brain then it's totally not hip. Seven out of ten don't survive it. So more or less, yes I had a stroke, by pure definition. Wikipedia: a stroke is a rapid loss of brain function(s) due to disturbance in the blood supply to the brain.

Some facts on strokes: They are the third most common cause of death in Germany. It is the most common cause for major disability. Strokes come in one of two flavours. A stroke can be either a red stroke or a white stroke. This colour code has a direct relation to the colour of the Brain, which is normally a greyish shade of pink.

Red strokes are when blood seeps into the brain colouring it red. Normally this means a burst blood vessel; they are also called haemorrhagic strokes and are split into two groups: intracerebral bleed (mine, ICB) or subarachnoidal, which is a bleed between skull bone and brain. These are often caused by an aneurism.

White strokes are due to a blood vessel being blocked, for example by a blood clot, also called ischaemic, embolic or thrombotic stroke. The area behind the blockage appears whiter than the usual pink thus the name. A white stroke can last several minutes and then disappear leaving no or only weak symptoms. This is called a transient stroke. This doesn't mean they're not dangerous even short transient ischeamic strokes in your brain stem can kill you off quickly and the vessel can also be blocked permanently having, worst case, the same effect.

A prolonged undernourishment can kill off brain cells resulting in the usual symptoms as well. Often both red and white come together, when a blood clot stops the blood flow (white), pressure rises and the affected vessel can pop (red). When a blood vessel pops the area behind this vessel can be undernourished. Both ways you're in trouble.

In Germany alone 150,000 to 200,000 people suffer a stroke of some kind each year. That's roughly one every three minutes. Of these, eighty five percent are white, mostly ischaemic which means a blockage. Fifteen percent are red intracerebral. Five percent are red subarachnoidal.

Brain surgery has come a long way in the last five years. I probably wouldn't have survived the same ordeal five years earlier. Again, that was impeccable timing by me. Although giant steps have been made in neurology, still 23,675 people didn't survive their stroke in 2009 and that's only in Germany. I am one of the lucky survivors.

Let's get back to things. After having to shake hands with my brain surgeon I was rolled into the operating room for my second try at brain surgery. This time the goal was the removal of the AVM. To do this you have to go in on a somewhat larger scale. So they removed a part of my skull, only to put it back afterwards fixed in place with a kind of pop rivet called a Craniofix. Three of them are in my head plus a small clip that holds the ends of my ruptured artery. All of them are made of some titanium alloy which is almost non-magnetic. (It's actually paramagnetic, but I'm not going explain that now; if it interests you, you can look it up yourself.)

So I don't beep when I go through metal detectors in airports but I should stay clear of super conducting high power electromagnets but that's ok because I don't work with those on a daily basis and no, I can't hear weird soviet radio stations or distant alien signals, there are only these strange voices telling me to eat more and more sausages... no worries, I just like wieners.

January 2012, a little more than two long years of uncertainty later, I found out that the second operation was successful. No residue. Two days after a contrast-agent angiogram, they fed a hollow wire into an artery in my groin; up through my heart all the way into my neck into the jugular artery where they injected the contrast-agent as close as possible to the brain and all this whilst fully conscious. While this was being done I was constantly being scanned so that the Surgeon didn't take a wrong turn and end up injecting the agent into my big toe. I could feel the wire about half way through my belly, and then the feeling dissipated. The contrast-agent, once injected gives off an uncanny feeling of wamth. Two days after that, as I sat in my wheelchair in the surgeons office, he came in and yelled "you're cured!" He quickly realised his error.

I said "Fine and I hope the cause is gone now." I mean I was sitting in front of him in a wheelchair, with my left side paralysed, far, far away from being "cured". He changed the subject quickly. If all of the AVM is removed it can't regrow. The odds of that is now not zero (they never are) but close enough to zero, to not have to worry about that anymore. (A death in traffic is definitely more probable, and I'm not by myself on that one.) More importantly they didn't find any other AVMs. So from his very special point of view the surgeon was sort of right, nonetheless, his comment was still a little tasteless. I also found out that the position of my rupture was quite easy to reach. This doesn't happen a lot. Most of the time, brain surgeons have to pierce through quite a bit of healthy brain tissue to get at the place causing the trouble, impairing brain functions that would normally remain intact. It's a matter of weighing up pro and contra. In my case there was no discussion, let me die or operate. So they operated. "Well it is pretty easy to get at, just a little bit through the motor cortex; we'll only make a small hole. He's right handed, that's good, and it'll only affect his left side. He's still young and will be able to cope with it." What a terrible job. I'd hate to carry that responsibility around with me all day.

"Hi, Honey, how was work today? Are the fresh veggies still in the car? "No dear, left them all in Intensive Care; you know I don't take work home with me."

A Big thanks to all the brain surgeons that had to cut me up. ‚Twas okay, no hard feelings, you had no choice, I'm still young and alive, and I'm going to cope.

Now there, I am getting way off track again. Back on track: So my brain is damaged from two haemorrhages and damaged some more by the surgeons, and so that no unneeded pressure can build up and the freshly clipped artery can go pop again, I really don't need to go through all that again.

So the brain is put into standby. They put me in an artificial coma for two months until everything had calmed down and healed. Fun opiates like Clonidin, Sufentanil and Propofol, the Michael Jackson killer. Whilst in a coma I almost had two Sepses (blood poisoning, 162 Deaths a day). They ruptured my right lung and let it collapse, more than a couple of pneumonias, a pseudomonas and a multi resistant Staphylococcus Aureus (MRSA).

Multi resistant means that most Antibiotics are useless against these germs. All but two of the worldwide obtainable broad band antibiotics weren't in my system and those that were are Chemical hydrogen bombs, those little resistant buggers eat normal stuff like penicillin for breakfast, on toast, with a cup o' coffee.

One other thing about artificial comas: you can't remember anything, nothing. Not a bit. Not even the opiate cold-turkey I went through, bathed in cold sweat, shivering. When I do something, I do it right. I go the whole nine yards. But it's all gone, don't remember a thing. Probably better that way.

But I can remember bits of the dreams and they were weird stuff. I fought in the Battle of Helm's deep out of Lord Of The Rings as an Ork. I even had the honour of being beheaded by Aragorn himself but only after having killed countless Rohans and elves. My goodness! did my breath smell bad? Dreams under opiates are unbelievably realistic.

In another dream, I was abducted by drunk female medical students who drove me to their after-finals party in an ambulance. They tied me naked to a giant wooden wheel and started throwing syringes at me like some giant rotating dart board. Just to keep the partying crowd amused.

Another, about the tree of life, which was hollow, the souls could drift up and down inside the hollow trunk. The souls went either down to Hell, or up to Valhalla in Asgard. My job was to help the poor souls to go up. There was a pretty complicated trade system about positive and negative energies and you could level up into higher planes of existence. It's a pity that I can't remember any details. It sounds like an interesting game concept.

I also stopped smoking while in the coma. Really easy, not even the slightest itch any more. I should patent it: two months artificial coma to become a non-smoker. It doesn't come any easier. Or does it?

I also bought all the microbes I had as plush-toys. No joke, they make toys from killer germs. I have a plush-MRSA and a plush-pneumonia. The shop didn't have a plush-pseudomonas but it looks almost the same as pneumonia so I just got two of them. They also have ebola, cholera and the plague but I haven't had those (and don't need to.) They also have normal stuff like bad breath and sore throat. Neurons were out of stock or I would have bought a truck load. (Just Google "giant microbes.") So if you ever wished your (ex) partner syphilis or gonorrhoea, you can send it as a present now. But keep me out of it!

Considering all these comatose horror stories, I was the only one who had an easy time. The people who really had a hard time were the ones nailed to my bedside. All the relatives and good friends that couldn't do anything but be there and wait. Will he wake up and if, how? Will he wake up as a veggie, with the mind of a chimp or a five year old without any memory? My brain haemorrhage was so large the neurologists weren't able to say much. I had the easy part. All I had to do was sit down in the back of the bus and enjoy the ride.

3. Dawn

From the neurological intensive care surgical ward I went into normal neurological intensive care. At first it was planned that I go directly to rehab but on my first trip from the UKE to the clinic in Hamburg Eilbek, I destroyed the innards of an ambulance and traumatised a doctor. Hey, I wasn't ready for the move, no one had asked nicely (I assumed no manners.) And they were going to take away the last of my drugs. I had to revolt.So my move was postponed a few days, weeks, whatever. Who am I to tell. Under opiates time is very relative, Kudos Einstein!

In Eilbek I "woke up" with a whole bunch of tubes coming out of my body. Trachea-tube in the neck, an in-dwelling venous catheter in the crook of my right arm for Clonidin, the last opiate they were still giving me, this in-dwelling venous catheter is like a valve to the venous system, used to take blood out of your system, put drugs in that way or hang me up to a drip infusion. It's a bit like the "Gardena" hose system with a similar amount of accessories. Also there was a urine catheter and a stomach tube through my abdominal wall to feed me with.

The "woke up" is in quotation marks on purpose because it wasn't like a normal, classical waking up after a good night's sleep. It was more like, hmm, it's difficult to explain to someone who hasn't experienced it. I'll try anyway: it's more like regaining consciousness over a very prolonged time. The Clonidin and other stuff were phased out over several weeks in the same time my consciousness was phased back in. there was no moment where I could say "I'm awake". Memory kicked back in very late and was still foggy, at the time when I was already in the early rehab ward. This is also the point where hearsay fades out and real memory kicks in. So everything after this point really happened, unless stated otherwise.

I have only memory fragments of Thomas, my first physiotherapist (he was right, the necessary work on the torso is being done now.) Something about making a bridge with my body and "keep going, four, three, two 'n' three quarters, two and a half, two, one, three…" Fred the male nurse kept cleaning me in shifts with uncountable nameless female nurses. I'm sorry, but you were all dressed in green steriles; I had no ability to (re)identify anyone let alone remember names. But thanks anyway.

There is one thing I remember quite well. I fell out of bed once. It was late and I was lying uncomfortably. So I grabbed the bed's remote control, fiddled around with it and then swoosh; it went over the side of the bed. I went after it. I wanted just a little look. Maybe it's stuck somewhere and I can get at it. I could not see it, so I went a little further, a little more, just a bit and somewhat more. Lean a bit over the edge. Blast! That's too much. Left arm useless, right arm went forward to break the fall. I went over the edge. Luckily I pulled the blanket with me, so I didn't get too cold during this ordeal. It was a really mean, unusually cold winter.

Unluckily the tube of the urine catheter wasn't long enough. Let me tell you how urine catheters work: simplified, they consist of a tube, actually two tubes, but we'll get to that later, with a bag on one end to collect the urine. The open end of the tube is inserted, with lots of lubricant into the urethra. It's inserted, as in my case, a male patient, through the penis up into the bladder. They are then blocked at the other end so the tube doesn't just slip out. The end of the tube has a balloon-thingy built into it and now we get back to the second tube through which the balloon is blown up with air to the size of a ping-pong ball.

Under no circumstances should one blow up the balloon while still in the urethra, for obvious reasons. The first tube goes through the balloon so that so the urine can trickle along and slowly fill up the bag on the other end of the tube. Because the bag end was tightly fastened to the other side of the bed and with my fall the slack tubing was very quickly used up and thus began a tug of war between the block and the bed. The bed won. And when the slack was gone, and the elasticity of the tube has reached equilibrium with the displacement of the balloon in the urethra, the block had become wedged right in the middle of, yeah, you guessed it!

There I was lying nicely tucked up with the tube strung taught and a ping-pong ball stuck right in the middle of my penis. The bell for the night nurse was incorporated in the remote control which I had pulled out of the wall while falling. Not just plug out of the socket but plug sheared off at the base, or else I could have plugged it back in. And the night nurse had just left the room, she had the whole ward to walk down and back again before coming back. Great! I couldn't even scream. I still had a tube going through my throat.

So I banged with the now totally useless and now very dead remote against a heating pipe. I was hoping that someone other than the sedated patients in the floors above and below me would hear me, and come looking. Somewhere in my childhood I had picked up "dot, dot, dot, dash, dash, dash, dot, dot, dot." Morse code for the international help signal: "SOS." I couldn't do anything else, so I sat there and watched the minutes tick on by... "Bangbangbang ... bang... bang... bang... bangbangbang." The clock mercifully didn't have a third hand that showed the seconds. Hours after painful hours later, about three quarters of an hour in real time, until they found me. All of sudden the room was crowded with countless numbers of these nameless nurses in uniform green. They heaved me back on the bed and cut the tube. But to no avail. Normally by cutting the tube logically, the air is let out of the balloon. But that didn't happen. Hmm, that's not so good. The nurses were clueless. They decided to wake up the Duty Urologist. He came and explained coolly the air couldn't escape. By stretching the tube, the inner diameter of the air-tube had shrunk to nothingness. The air can't get through. "Look here, you can see it clearly on the cut off end. Look here". He held up the cut off tube, showing it to the nurses in a matter of fact way, meaning: "you woke me up for this?"

But, what can we do now? Where does that leave me? "This is going to hurt a bit." he said, and before I could react he grabbed a pair of pliers, got a hold of the short stub of tubing left hanging out of me and pulled. Humans aren't made to cope with such pain. I Pissed blood for three days. No further comment. Only one thing, I never fell out of bed again.

Strange was also the occasional disorientation. Sometimes I woke up in a different room, I mean, different to the room I had gone to bed in, or so it seemed. As soon as I was able to describe the old room, we found out that the room had been in the UKE. No worries, These flashbacks are not uncommon with neurological patients, especially in connection with high opiate dosages like the ones I was getting. The real question was that I had never seen the UKE from the inside on a conscious level. I still have no conscious memory after the second bleed. So why could I describe the mountains of monitoring equipment towering over my head. Maybe something does get through the coma on some subconscious level. But who knows, maybe I was just dreaming episodes of "Dr. House."Brains are wierd stuff.

So they taught me how to breathe by myself again. Slowly reducing the extra oxygen I needed. That's pretty complicated stuff. Not the reducing. You reduce the oxygen by just turning a knob. It's the breathing that isn't easy, especially if you are breathing through a small tube that's sticking out of the front of your neck and constantly scratching at the back of your windpipe.

Tracheotomy tubes are blocked like urine catheters, only that the balloon is blown up in your windpipe instead of your bladder. There is no other way to get air to your lungs. You have no choice but to breathe through the pipe in your neck.

Downside is that your saliva gathers in the tube above the block and after a while, in my case around twenty minutes. Depending on your rate of slavering at some point you start to make blubbering noises, with the effect that you have to call a nurse who then clears the tube of saliva. A large portion of my time was spent ringing, waiting for a nurse to come, then pointing at my throat making gurgling noises, indicating that I needed to have my tube cleared. Sometime later I'd relearned breathing and the extra oxygen wasn't necessary anymore. My oxygen saturation was still monitored the whole time by a clamp on my finger that kept slipping off, constantly setting off uncountable false alarms.

Above my bed was a photo of my brother, he's a bit wider than I am. He's not fat; he's got a lot more muscle mass than I do. He's a little smaller, but wider, more compact than I am. He's a metalworker, he needs it. I work at a desk, I don't. Anyway it came to a little mix-up and the hospital staff thought it was me on the photo. "Oh my, has he lost weight, didn't they feed him at all in the UKE. The poor thing!" So they upped the calories. To 3000 kcal per day! After my mum found out, she cleared the situation and my feeding was toned down to 1700 kcal again, which is still a lot if all you do is lie around in bed all day. It was probably necessary because I weighed less than sixty kilos at the time. At the moment I'm fighting the eighty down to seventy again, which is normal for me. But I still use the forced feeding as an excuse when someone comments on my little belly, although I expect it's got more to do with my consumption of fast food, namely delivered pizza and burgers, but please don't tell anyone!

With a hole in your throat you can't speak. I wrote the whole time. At first they gave me a piece of laminated cardboard with letters on it. Sender, me, points at "A" receiver says "A", sender gives a thumbs up or nods, next letter. By the time you communicate: "I'd like to eat a banana please," you could have taught the banana to speak it. And the piece of cardboard didn't even have a keyboard layout it went "ABCDE" and not "QWERT" so you even had to search for the letters prolonging things even further. So I made writing gestures with my healthy right hand. It took awhile and my mum was the first to get it. I wanted pen and paper and not some stupid makeshift keyboard. She ripped out the last page of her book, which was conveniently left blank, a nurse had a pen. And so I started communicating again. The first thing I wrote was: "this smells like opiates", the second: "get that man a puzzle". My elderly roommate was terribly bored and always started taking things apart, including his tubing, which often ended with him bleeding out of diverse orifices. Before this point nobody knew the state of my mind. Well I was back! Cognitive functions fully active and ready to rock and roll. Much to everyone's surprise. Even the hospital staff, neurologists included, were bewildered. It seems my brain haemorrhage was so massive that not much was expected. But I definitely thought otherwise. And I still believe you can smell opiates, but ask drug dogs they have more experience in that than me.

Next in line was swallowing. Even more complicated than breathing. An extraordinary number of muscles need to be switched on and off in the exact right order: Chew phase, collect the chewed food in the front of your mouth, close the nasal cavities off, lift your larynx which closes your trachea with your epiglottis, "roll" the chewed food with your tongue to your oesophagus in a wavelike motion, push it down into the upper part of the oesophagus and start breathing again. Take the next bite and repeat. Make a mistake in the order of, or a slip in the timing, you hit your windpipe and choke.

Liquids are hardest because they are so quick in getting to the back of your mouth. I must have breathed litres of water. That's why you start off with a drop of tea on the tongue moving on slowly through jelly, to mash, to more solid stuff. Peas are bad! They roll! Peas in your windpipe are not funny. Patting on the back doesn't help, it just distracts. Normally if you don't panic and breathe out heavily, the peas fly out again. You can survive several minutes without breathing before your brain is damaged. The rest of your body will recover easily. Try it in the bathtub! But don't overdo it. On second thought, don't. Don't even go near the tub, it's dangerous and can kill you! Brain damage isn't fun. Believe me; I know all about that firsthand.

Another difficult thing to do with a tube in your neck is speaking. You can't! With a blocked tube in your windpipe you can't get air from your lungs to your vocal chords. So you get a special tube that has an adapter, which can accommodate different extras. One of these extras is a membrane, which simulates vocal chords. It's a very disturbing experience when your voice is created not in, but completely outside your own throat. You still try to modulate your voice by using your tongue and lips, but that is totally useless because the vibrations are generated somewhere outside your head. At first you just make strange noises that no one can understand, not even you. With a lot of practise at some point you begin to understand yourself again. Not much later even others can understand you. This happens almost parallel to learning swallowing and as soon as both were finished they removed my trachea-tubing.

Being allowed to eat again my friends organised a barbeque. In the middle of that nasty winter they bought a gas fired grill and grilled burgers on the front lawn of the clinic in fifteen centimetres of snow and ice. They smoked out the whole building but the burgers were great, just a tad bloodier than medium which is what burgers are all about, and no useless salad stuff, just a wad of meat and a thin slice of aged cheddar. Maybe just a hint of homemade smoked barbeque sauce. No more. I ate two and was very dissappointed that I could eat no more. Perfect, guys!

My grandpa died when I was in coma. Bad as it was he left us with somewhat of a large debt to remember him by. Everyone else had turned down the inheritance except me, and so I was the last one and about to inherit, with time running out. "No, Mrs. Herzberg, your husband must sign personally, even if he's still in intensive care and just out of coma. And no, your legal custodianship isn't enough. If he's conscious, he must sign himself, and of course in the presence of a notary." Signing wasn't the problem. The problem was: I was still on intensive care. At this point There were still tubes sticking out of me. So I wasn't going anywhere fast.

At this point they were still monitoring the oxygen saturation level of my blood, amongst other vital functions. So the notary of Hamburg's most renowned lawyer's office had to come to me. Also, my ward wasn't only intensive care, but I was also under strict quarantine because of several nasty germs already mentioned. Everyone had to cover up in a sterile plastic overcoat, gloves, face mask and head cover. Even the little blue plastic shoe covers. You also had to all but bathe in sterilising agents. And the notary had to go through this procedure. As did every nurse, doctor and visitor, everyone had to. No excuses because of biohazard protocols. He came. He hesitated ever so slightly as he did not shake my offered hand. I signed. He left, very quickly. I'd never seen a notary almost run. Notaries are paid by the hour, he didn't care.

Speaking of germs as soon as I had gotten rid of the Notary, the staff had to act fast. They didn't want to risk me getting infected again by touching my old pencil. So everything that couldn't be sterilised or wasn't worth sterilising was destroyed. My pencil did the latter. Meanwhile I was put into my first wheelchair; we called it my rolling lounge. It was a huge, very comfortable affair, with a headrest, bottle holder and a little collapsible table. I was rolled into the hallway while my room was being dismantled and cleaned. MRSA and pseudomonas aren't dangerous to normal, healthy people. You're probably carrying them with you at the moment but your immune system is holding them back the whole time. Unfortunately my immune system was busy fighting open wounds like my tracheostoma and my stomach tube, micro infections at my urine catheter, not to mention coping with the residue of heavy opiates, antibiotics, anticoagulants and muscle relaxants, not to mention what was being repaired, reabsorbed, and reconnected in my brain. So these germs were very dangerous for me. But they didn't break out. Lucky me, again!

My new roommate Mr. Mueller (name changed by the author) who watched TV until way into the night only to fall asleep with his headphones blaring, keeping me awake. Every night I would ring for up the night nurse, who then switched off the TV, put the remote in the drawer of his bedside table, removed his headphones, stowed them in the same drawer, wished me a good night and switched the light off. She did this with an almost stoic composure that was admirable. It became a ritual. At daytime I also had to call a nurse for him because his tracheostomy tube filled up quicker than mine. So when he started bubbling, RRRiiiinngg, "what's up?" "Mueller's drowning." "Again?" You're thinking: "why didn't he call himself", right? That's because his arms were bandaged fast from his fingertips to his elbows to stop him pulling out his tubing. Dementia is a bitch.

Now that we had conquered the enemy germs it was time to move from early rehab into real rehab. As a patient you don't really have a good sense of time. Every day is pretty much the same as any other day. You don't really have a weekend, and there were no significant landmarks along the way. The days were monotonous, differing little. I couldn't be able to tell which day of the week it was. But then again, it didn't really matter.

So I was mildly surprised by the two paramedics standing next to my bed one day.

I asked "what's up?"

"We are goin' to remove your stomach tube." Well, well, I was in for a bit of action today. 'Bout time. I was transferred to a mobile bed and rolled to an ambulance, stashed into the back, the doors were closed and off we went! After about a six hundred meter ride around the building we stopped again. I was pulled back out and rolled back into another entrance of the same building. Believe me. I'm still confused about that one.

Insurance reasons, germ territory or worse, stairs, could all have been reasons for the ambulance! I could only guess. I asked the medics but they had been told to take me from A to B, no more. They were as clueless as I was. I was then transferred back into a bed. After waiting a while a nurse came to pick me up. She rolled me into an examination room. The walls were covered with screens.

A doctor came in and told me what was going to happen. My stomach tube went through my abdominal wall into my stomach; it went through a small plastic tile where it was secured with a nut. All that was going to happen was that he would use an endoscope down my throat to find the tile, remove the nut and the plastic tile and pull the tube out. It was that easy? Cool, I thought. I already had a good view of the screens and leaned back to enjoy the show.

I signed the obligatory certificate of non-objection. Yes I know that I can die of complications even during simple intrusions. No, I will not sue you or the hospital if anything goes wrong. If I'm dead, I can't do that, if I survive there's no reason to. They gave me a venous catheter, just for the unlikely chance of an emergency. They always do that. I'm already used to it. The crook of my right arm was dotted with holes and resulting bruises. But instead of grabbing the endoscope, first he injects something into my catheter. I thought probably something to suppress the faucal reflex. That's ok; I didn't want to throw up either. Seeming satisfied, he left ... And never came back. Ten minutes later, the Medics came with their mobile bed.

"Wrong room guys, " I said. "We haven't even started yet."

"That's what they all say," replied one of them, with a smile on his face. I didn't believe it until I saw the rapidly closing hole, which the tube had left in my belly. It wasn't a vomiting suppressant it was a quick and yet subtle anaesthetic. They'd knocked me out! That's what you get for not reading the fine print on things you sign. So I missed the show. I went back to the other side of the clinic again in the ambulance.

For me, in an indeterminable span of time later, it could have been days/weeks/months, two other paramedics stood beside my bed. This time I had an idea what was happening. My wife had been packing my stuff all day. And off I was! It was time for a bigger move. Bye bye Eilbek, welcome to Gesthacht!

4. Good morning

I could have landed up in the nowhere of Bavaria, (It's pretty much the same sending someone from New York to Nebraska or from Sydney to Coolgardie. It'll cause cultural shock; on both sides. You just don't do it!) In Bavaria I would have had more treatments per week, which would have been good, but I wouldn't have understood anyone. The dialect is so different, I might as well have gone to, let's say Finland. The clinic in Bavaria, one in Bad Segeberg and Geesthacht (both in northern Germany) were suggested by my health insurance. Geesthacht made the race because the clinic was for young people. That was much better than alphorns and dirndls.

Residing in an old tuberculosis clinic a mix of "general hospital" and the Overlook Hotel from Stephen King's "Shining", lots of long empty corridors bathed in the pale, eerie green glow of the not too distant nuclear power plant Kruemmel. (Not really, for one, uranium glows blue, not green in heavy water also second, Kruemmel had been switched off for maintenance and security reasons several months earlier.)

In Geesthacht I finished lots of the work started in Eilbek. They tortured me with the same physical and cognitive ordeals. First goal was the transfer from bed to wheelchair. I ticked that one off pretty quickly so I could go to the toilet on my own. This was followed by learning to put on clothes again with only one functioning arm and leg. Sometimes my tee-shirts still get caught on my left shoulder, but I can live with that, and I still can't tie my shoes. Velcro rules!

I also did a lot of work just standing, it's good for posture and balance. I also had to fight my pes equinus. (Ok, Latin medical term, I'll explain: because of the high muscular tone my left foot was always stretched, much like a ballerina, this does a whole bunch of bad things to the muscles, sinews and bones. The easiest way to compensate this was standing on it.)

At first I stood only under supervision in therapy. Later I stood on the balcony that went off from the patient's kitchen, where they had a bar at above breast height to stop suicidal patients from jumping! No joke! We had several "incidents", no jumpers, but other attempts. Thankfully none were successful. But it was perfect to hold on to and start walking again from side to side.

Wait a sec ... I just remember toppling over once. There was a little ridge in the doorway from kitchen to balcony that I had to get over. This wasn't really a problem. You move the front wheels of the wheelchair so they are just touching the ridge. Then your jerk the big wheels forward so that the little wheels rise up above the ridge; the momentum generated by the jerk will the carry the front wheels over the ridge. Then you heave the back wheels over the ridge by sheer force.

Sounds easy enough, there's only one problem. If you jerk too hard the front wheels will rise too high. The momentum will then topple you onto your back. The wheelchair does a back flip. In the worst case it'll end up on top of you. To stop this happening there is a safety wheel, which is flipped out the back and bottom of the wheelchair. Before you do a backflip it hits the ground and stops your extra momentum. This works fine, presuming it is snapped out. Which it always is, except this one fine morning! I jerked the wheels and...

"Wait, that's too far!" Then you have this temporally decoupled moment of weightlessness at the point of no return.

"Shit!" ... you keep going; pull down your head as a reflex. Bang! I was saved from fracturing my skull by the handles of the wheelchair. And once again, this happened only once to me. As a rule I only do frightening, sickening, painful and life threatening things once. Works fine for me.

There was a small inconspicuous grey box up on the outside wall of the balcony with a power line feeding out of it, going down then through the wall into the bowels of the kitchen. I can't remember who it was but someone said that this must be the anti-elephant field generator. You don't believe me? Well I was there one and a half years and didn't see even one elephant. So it must work pretty well.

Training wasn't just done in therapy and on the balcony. In the evening, when things had quietened down, we stole down into the therapy wing where there was a corridor with a handrail at the right height. I went up and down, up and down with the whips of my wife and mother on my heels.

They found out that you could rent rooms in the clinic, which they did, so that they could torture me fulltime.

There was also a load of cognitive training, loads of math and puzzle stuff. We played games to test and strengthen my memory. I did tons of eye work to help me compensate my probably permanent field of vision impairment in the lower left quadrant of sight. I was now wearing glasses. I was doing this to get back into a state that I could go back to work. The visual impairment is difficult to explain and I'm still not sure if I've got it right. The eye isn't physically damaged at all, and I had better than twenty-twenty vision beforehand. It's the optical nerve or the area processing the imagery that's been damaged. Now the world is out of focus. How glasses help is still a complete mystery to me. No one has been able to supply a sufficient explanation. In addition to that a portion of the lower left quadrant is gone. Well sort of. The brain only directly processes the area we directly focus on; the rest of the complete image is put together by unfocused and older focussed imagery. In this area we can only detect motion. The brain is pretty clever; this saves a lot of processing bandwidth compared to processing the whole image. But this is just a simplified version.

Neural image processing is a lot more complicated than that. Anyway, either the transfer to this temporary image is impaired, or the memory banks holding this image are too slow or broken. If I focus in that region everything's normal. So now have to scan the lower left actively to make sure if there's nothing dangerous like tigers, snakes or crocs coming for me from that angle. Any which way, the Big Picture isn't up to date the whole time. I don't pick up movement fast enough and run into quick things that creep up on the lower left of me. Chairs, tables, rubbish bins, you name it, I've kicked it.

That's the reason why they took away my driver's licence. I was at the Vehicle Enforcement Authority to pick up my Handicapped Parking ID.

"Hey, you can't drive!" They said. I was sitting in my wheelchair.

"I'm not going to." I replied.

"Doesn't matter, hand over your licence, and I'm afraid you'll have to pay the service fee of 160 Euros." They said.

I didn't argue. No use, I paid. I could have filed a complaint which would have taken hours of precious time, probably fill out hundreds upon hundreds of forms, have my financial background checked, waited months for an answer only to pay anyway. Sometimes it's easier to shut up and let it be. It's only money. And like I said I'm not going to drive anyway. So I don't really need that licence. That's way too dangerous for me and my environment.

For some time the doctors talked about my neglect, and I mixed that up with my field of vision problem. That's because the symptoms overlap. With neglect on the left side you don't perceive things on the left side, you see them very clearly but they are not heaved to a conscious level. You simply don't notice things. People always surprise me when they come from the left. That's only if I notice them at all. Good thing they took away my driver's licence. That can be dangerous filing in on the Autobahn going at over 150 kilometres an hour. It's a communication problem between consciousness and subconsciousness. Example: There I am on my way to the toilet going fast as I can. I'm in a hurry, pressure is building up, and I need to pee badly. On the way my left shoulder hits the frame of the door, hard.

"Ow, that hurt, why didn't you warn me?" Says conscious to subconscious, "Were you asleep again?"

"I did, just a second ago, watch it, door frame! Why didn't you look yourself?" Replies Subconscious.

"No, you didn't! And I didn't because I'm busy walking and keeping things in balance. These are, incidentally, supposed to be your jobs too! "

"Typical, you never listen to me!"

"Who'd want listen to your chatter all day long anyway. Tell you the truth I have to filter 99 percent of it away. Anyhow it's all in black and white in the contract. Didn't you read the fine print?" "Ha, See, you really never listen." Sort of like a married couple.

The neglect can impair all five senses in my case it's just the optical and the sense of touch. Only about thirty percent of all stimuli come through to a conscious level this is great when someone is sticking needles or syringes into you. Bad when your wife touches you and all you get is a nasty ticklish feeling. It isn't like being numb; it all gets to me, just at a third of its normal level. So it's more or less a volume issue. What a pity that it's not possible to repair the connection. Damaged brain tissue stays damaged. Other parts of the brain have to learn this all anew and that takes time. There is nothing you can do to speed it up except repetition. So I learn patience.

My sense of taste isn't damaged. The food in Geesthacht was way better than Eilbek. They even have their own cooks and all. This isn't normal in clinics this size. Normally the cooking is outsourced to a large catering kitchen which then delivers the food in gastro norm containers that only need heating to be served. In Geesthacht a lot was from deep frozen produce but they were always mixed with fresh vegetables. The meat was grilled not deep-fried or even worse, steamed. There was a salad bar and always, fresh fruit. My dishes were always of somewhat larger size. The people behind the counter quickly gave me my ten pancakes so that I didn't have to line up again for seconds or thirds. It was a pity that the menu rotated every five weeks, as a long-term inmate you pick up on that pretty soon. Did I mention that the pancakes were fantastic? As was the Christmas dinner.

The head of the clinic organised a Michélin starred chef to make us a four-course meal with his apprentices. What a terrific meal. Oh yes, and the Pancakes were really good too!

The snoozelen room (Dutch I assume) was unbelievable. It was a whole room just to relax. We even had a therapy there simply called "relaxing." We did guided meditation and autogenic training. Or just listened to spacey ambient music lying on the heated waterbed with the integrated subwoofers or lounged in a bean bag watching the bubbles go up in liquid filled tubes or looked at the weird reflections the rotating disco ball threw at the wall from the spots that flickered to the music. Soon I had a nickname: "the snorer" because I fell asleep more than once. Although I don't really snore, it's more a nasal wheeze.

Even better was that you could borrow the key to the room from ward A. (I was in B.) So I could even relax after hours.

I had loads of visitors. My brother and sister came extra from Australia. My mum and wife were there almost all the time taking shifts. And of course friends and family came weekends to breakfast or brunch. Not all visitors were good. Once I was visited by an evaluator sent from court. She was there to check if I was certifiably sane and in possession of all my wits again. My wife and mother still my legal custodians and I wanted to get rid of that. I put on a white shirt (have you ever tried buttoning with one hand, it's very difficult.) So she came, we talked and then came the big one:

"Are you still potent?" She asked.

"????? ... ??? ... !!! ... ?????" I was bewildered. My eyes must have expressed this clearly. She picked up her bag.

"What's this got to do with my brain haemorrhage?" I returned slightly aggravated. She went quickly. She left me utterly confused. I'm still not sure if that was part of the test or not. Afterwards I informed a nurse and the clinic filed a formal complaint at court against this intriguingly unusual style of evaluation. Soon I was back to being a full legal citizen with all my rights. Oh, I almost forgot, the court billed me anyway.

The therapists prescribe lots of aids and not all are covered by health insurance. One tool was a cradle knife for one-handed people. Denied: "Even normal people have to buy new knives every now and then." Anti-slip mats. Denied again. Guess what:" you can also buy placemats every now and again." I bought what I needed myself.

Approved were all the medical things. Diverse Arm and leg braces to literally put me back into form. One we called my "tube" it was like a glove that went over the elbow. It helped against my neglect stimulating the perception of my skin by applying constant pressure to my hand and arm. Constant stimuli are even better than repeated stimulation. It was sewn in Ireland by hand. My exact hand and arm measurements were taken and sent away.

I imagined green rolling hills and a dark grey sky, darkening towards the horizon foreboding even worse weather. There on a hill of grass stood a little grey weather-beaten, wooden shack in the dead centre of nowhere special. A cold, never-ending wind whistling through the gaps in the planking of the walls. The shingles on the roof clattering to an unknown avant-garde rhythm. The single room is dominated by a black peat fired oven. The flickering red glow of the receding fire casts eerie shadows through the bent grate onto the fading pictures on the opposing wall. They were remnants of happier times long gone by. Although old the oven gives off constant warmth for the bent over "Seamstress" sitting on a three-legged stool listening to the beginning rain spattering against the only blackened window. She sits there in the dim reddish light checking my measurements while she sews my glove with a precision you can only gain by the sewing experience gained in three quarters of a century but she's complacent and content because she knows it's another job well done.

You think that's too romantic? You're probably right, the office in lower Belfast probably gave the job to the cheapest Chinese factory with supervisors with whips, beating the children working for a morsel of food, but they definitely did it cheaper and faster. But please leave me my illusions. Anyway it fitted so tight that it was very difficult to put on.

Worse was a brace that was made to help against my above-mentioned pes equines. It held the foot tight in a polyurethane cast with the upper end tied to my calf. So you could then force the angle of the foot to the leg and fasten it in an angle that was closer to the normal right angle than my muscles and sinews would allow by themselves. I even had to sleep with this contraption. I'm usually more the active sleeper, constantly trying to find a more comfortable position while falling asleep. That's hard to do with a five-kilo brace strapped to your leg. Only being able to sleep on my back was pure torture. I had a couple of sleepless nights, grew grumpy until the doctors had had enough of my bickering, with the result that I only had to wear the thing at day. Like I said, standing was more effective and soon the brace landed in a corner of my cupboard. Just a note: I refrained from taking sleep-inducing pills the whole time.

The clinic also had a Lokomat. And no this thing isn't a gone crazy washing machine or a model railway in H0. It's a huge walking machine. I was strapped into a large frame. My legs were tied fast to the legs of the machine then I was heaved up so that my legs didn't have to carry my own weight anymore. It was very important that my groin was well cushioned so that the straps of fabric holding me up didn't dig into my flesh. And then the thing started to walk with me securely fastened into it. At first, with my legs dangling in the air, until I got into the flow of it. This sounds easier than it was, when all the muscles in my left leg went stiff on me, not allowing my knee to bend at all. When the machine measures too much resistance a safety mechanism automatically stops it. I didn't want to be in the vicinity if the safety failed and bones could have been crunched, joints burst and muscles ripped apart.

Most of the time, I got into the rhythm, going with, and not against the machine as I was lowered onto the conveyor belt, which was running under me, putting weight back onto my feet. The walk was physiologically correct right down to rolling correctly off my heel and toes. I could even change the speed of it. I never got over one and a half kilometres an hour.

Sounds easy? It isn't! For one: it was chafing my ankles and groin time after time. Second: when walking you normally put in little bits of rest automatically, the machine didn't. It just went on, and on, and on, and on. No pause.

Just you and the relentless robotic thing: walking, walking, walking and walking. I began to feel like a hamster in its running wheel. I did this for half an hour and was spent, bathed in sweat. Yearning to get back in to my comfy wheelchair and just sit. I'm not even sure if it helped. I think it was a little too early for me to get maximum benefit out of it. It didn't do me any harm so I guess it was ok. I think I'll have another go at it when my left knee plays along.

My technical environment was first rate, I had an iPod touch to hear music, a small netbook with built in 3G flatrate for surfing on the Internet (it's great to have friends in high places in the mobile business.) iPad and Amazon kindle came late and of course a full HD LCD TV with Blue-Ray player. My little sisters gave me that one. So I was never bored.

I also had to swim. I hated that. It's not that I can't, because I can, or better, could. It's just that when my left side is paralysed I was in constant fear of drowning even if there was a therapist at arm's length watching out for me. Even the thought of large bodies of water made my stress level rise. When this happened, the muscle tone in my left side would reach unimaginable levels.

There are two types of spasticity. One has a high muscle tone the other low or no muscle tone. Either type, I couldn't control the affected muscles, because, in my case the high muscle tone variant was in the whole left half of my body. When I'm standing and not holding onto something very solid, there's already enough stress to provoke a reaction. The muscles in my left extremities go haywire. They play a game of tug of war with each other.

Most muscles have a counterpart, i.e. one to bend your knee (calf) one to stretch it. The stronger muscle wins. In my leg, the quadriceps femoralis (the four headed monster in the front of the thigh, from kneecap to groin, one of the strongest muscles in the body wins, pulling the leg straight, with such force, that no one else, no matter how strong, can bend it. Only by tearing a muscle or sinew could the leg be straightened.

In my arm the biceps wins. It's stronger than its counterpart the triceps, by a long shot. This pulls the arm up against my chest. My left hand is almost always fully clenched. The muscles making the fist are way stronger than the ones to open it.

Even the muscles in the face are affected. My face snarls uncontrollably when I'm stressed. This has the effect that the winning muscles and their sinews get stronger and stronger; the weaker ones degenerate and shorten. The higher the stress level the worse it gets. Sometimes it ends in a tremor when the muscles fire erratically. It looks really spooky but it isn't dangerous. I apply a little pressure: put weight on the leg or press the fist against some hard object and the tremors dissipate. It doesn't hurt and looks like a seizure.

When I'm asleep there is little or no muscular tone. Same when I meditate. Then the weaker muscles have a chance and go for it: bending my leg and straightening my arm. That's the reason why my weaker muscles haven't atrophied. Both directions are trained, one way or the other.

For some people, swimming in water has the exact opposite effect. They can let go and their high muscle tone is almost gone and they learn to gain control that way again. Not me! I never take the easy road. Why should I? It's almost like cheating. I'm glad for those that can. Swimming was taken off my timetable leaving more time for other therapy.

At some time I could walk a small distance with a crutch, although I still spent most of my time in my wheelchair. Everyone was saying "patience" which incidentally was named my personal taboo word of the year 2011. 2010 it was "insurance." 2012 hasn't been decided yet the two hot candidates are "torso" and "therapist," with "torso" leading ever so slightly.

About 9 Months after day zero my wife and I were driving in the vicinity of our flat. By this time I was allowed to leave the clinic on weekends. I besieged my wife to drive past my home, so I could have a look at it. I hadn't been home in all this time because we live on the third floor with no lift. What my wife didn't know was that I'd been practicing stairs for some weeks when she was at work and not in the clinic. I wasn't really good at it and my therapists would have killed me for trying, but who gives: No risk no fun! So up I went. Finally at the top, I'd never done three stories before, bathed in sweat, gasping for air. My wife just stood there gaping like a goldfish. Not believing what had just happened. As soon as she had control of herself again, she phoned up all of our friends: "Come on over. Tim's back!" We had a very nice spontaneous homecoming party. I also got back down again. (I'd practiced that too.) I had to be back before the doors of the clinic closed at ten PM. We just made it and I grinned like a daft monkey for the next couple of days.

We even had a treadmill delivered to my room in the clinic so I could train in the afternoons after my clinic timetable had ended. That probably sounds like really ambitious, totally aspiring, and great drive and from the outside this is what it may have looked like. In the clinic I have this reputation: I may not look it, but to tell you the truth, I'm a lazy slob that you have to kick twice before anything happens.

Don't get me wrong. I understood perfectly well that I had to work to get back on my feet. But in the afternoon after therapy I was so done with, that all I wanted to do was sleep. So my beloved wife and loving mother put me to work in the evenings after my siesta. In retrospect it was probably good that way. Although I was driven close to madness, I recuperated faster than anyone else had. By the way, I've kept the siesta and ditched most of the extra work. Like I said: lazy slob!

My typical day went like this: Seven AM, an awake call by the nurse on duty for my room. Off to breakfast. Wait! First get dressed. If my leg is willing, put trousers on by myself. If not, call for help. If the leg is already straight I had no chance. Same goes for the shoes. It took almost a year for the leg to become pliable enough for me to do this myself on a daily basis and I still had days where it didn't want to play. Next: tee-shirt. Find the left sleeve, feed my right arm down it into the bottom, grab my left hand pull the shirt over my left arm, pull my head through the hole at the top, right arm is easy. The tee-shirt keeps tangling up with my left shoulder so I have to pull it over the shoulder and then straighten it.

I check my timetable, typical day: double session physiotherapy, cognitive training, lunch, speech therapy, swimming. Physiotherapy first, I go down into the torture chambers in the basement. Wait. Almost forgot my morning pills. I swallow them dry, it's quicker. Time is running out. The corridors are filled with crutches, rollers, lurchers waiting for the march-in of the therapists. They had a prolonged morning mission briefing. There was couple-building going on. Patient finds therapist and vice versa. The chaos lessens as the couples disappear into rooms to left and right.

Two therapists are left standing. Two patients are missing. Quick check with ward clears the situation. The two fourteen year olds are too "cool" to get up. The Therapists give each other a quick nod and head up to the ward, for a more rigorous wake up, "happens all the time," they say. "Teenagers! Don't know what's good for them."

After Physio, It's cognitive training. Believe me; this can be more exhausting than physical training. We play a game: Subject is animals: Let's start with "cat" the next person has to name an animal starting with last letter of the word before so "tiger" would be allowed as would "tarantula"... "Armadillo" ... "Ostrich"... "Horse" ..."Echidna," and so on. You are not to use a word twice, inhibiting cyclic word building: "Rat"… "Tapir"… "Rat" … or "Eagle" … "Eagle" … "Eagle" … It isn't as easy as you think. And if you really run out of words try changing the subject: "tools," "diseases," "vegetables," "cities." Try rotating subjects, first a carnivore, a flower, an insect and back to carnivore. Use your imagination. It's a simple game, but it keeps your mind flexible. This is what cognitive training is all about.

I already had a look at the lunch menu at breakfast: Yeast dumpling filled with plum sauce. That's almost as good as pancakes. Did I tell you? … Yes, I think I did. Mess hall is on first floor. So I take the elevator out of the basement to ground level. Roll through half the length of the building only to find that I'm at the end of line. Again.

There's an elevator that takes you to the last floor up to the mess hall and it can only take one wheelchair at a time. With half the clinic inmates dependant on wheelchairs or the like, this is pretty much a bottleneck situation every breakfast, lunch and dinner. So you wait your turn. Line up at the counter and then order: Three dumplings! I'm not all too hungry and no swimming with a full stomach. I usually do four. I Tried five once, they almost killed me. If I'm fast and get back to my room with no bigger hassles on the way, I can digest and take a half hour nap.

Off I go. Back down the slow single wheelchair elevator, skip the smaller first elevator, two people are already waiting, take the big one which means I roll a couple of hundred meters longer but it's faster and if someone's waiting we'll both fit in. Up to second floor where my ward is on, off to my room.

There's a note on my pillow: Swimming is off! Great! I really hate swimming! I find out later that some little toddler had an "accident". This happens quite often even with waterproof diapers. Good for me, bad for the cleaning crews. Off to bed, for half an hour of rest. Set the alarm to countdown. Beep … Beep … Beep. The Alarm goes off.

It's time for speech training. This time I'm prepared: My wife and I actually practiced this time. We spent half the night talking with a cork jammed between the incisors, which made us sound stupid, and made us look even more so, but it is intensive training for the ring muscle around the mouth. It improves articulation. By the way, I still can't whistle properly, a little air escapes on the left corner. But I'm working on it.

After therapy I'm free to do what I want. Siesta-time! Set the alarm to seven. Go to dinner, just some bread with cheese; the dumplings are still not digested. Go to the nurses' room to pick up my evening medication. Don't forget to brush your teeth, maybe watch a little TV. Goodnight. See you in the morning.

One morning I woke up and my roommate Tony was missing, not only Tony, but all his stuff too! Even his bed was gone. Did they move him last night? Did someone paint the ceiling over night? It wasn't its usual light pink (I know, and yes, in Geesthacht they put me in a girls room, believe me, worse has happend to me.) "Must be a trick of the light, "I thought. You're still sleepy. Hmm. Something wrong with my toungue. Oww. Pain strikes me as I ispect it. And why have I got a venous catheter in the crook of my arm? It's all very mysterious. Questions start to swirl and form in my mind, not connecting yet. A nurse comes in. Strange never seen her before. Nice, but I've seen nicer. And I know all the nurses in Geesthacht, but she's not one. That's all very strange.

"Good Morning Mr. Herzberg. Nice to see you awake. You've had an epileptic grand mal seizure and you're in the UKE because in Geesthacht they couldn't get you out of it. We had to give you Valium intravenously to stop your convulsing; oh, you bit your tongue whilst at it. No, don't fiddle with it, there's nothing missing but you can clearly see your bite marks on it. It's going to hurt for a couple of days. Gargle with this." She held up a bottle."You've been here two days; we've scanned you again to see if everything's okay and it is. No new bleeding at all. We'll send you back to Geesthacht today. Do you have any questions?" Off she went.

Questions? None and thousands. Why do I have to hit every rock that's on my road? Why can't I miss just one? Epilepsy, great what's next? … Bring it on. I'll take it all.

It seems that I had a seizure while phoning with my wife. One moment there I am talking to my wife about whatever (can't remember a thing). The next moment I was lying on the floor jerking this way and that. I bit my tongue and plastered the wall with my blood. Tony had alerted the nurses and they had called an ambulance suspecting or fearing new brain haemorrhage. My wife was almost quicker and she had forty kilometres and not five to drive.

They suspected that I'd already had smaller seizures. The night nurse thought she had seen me cramping at times. But they could have just been bad dreams. Weird spasms are normal for me. They could be epileptic and come about twice a day. But they are minor tremors and totally harmless.

Epileptic seizures are normally harmless too, unless you bite your tongue or hurt yourself falling, nothing bad happens. You're just knocked out as the electric cascade rattles your brain. When this is over and the cascade dissipates, you wake up with no memory of it. If you find someone having a seizure, there's not much you can do, unless you have 2.5 mg sublingual Tavor at hand, which you won't. Just cushion the head and keep the patient from hurting themselves. Calling an ambulance is always a good idea.

I take medication against that now and haven't had a new seizure in almost two years. Regular EEGs show nothing suspicious. The drug is a new one called Keppra, which in my case has no side effects and no one knows how it works. It's not that it doesn't. It works fine it's just that no one knows how.

Some people get ... dam 'it. Get away from me. I bite! One more step and I'll whack you with my crutch... aggressive. Not me. Calm as a kitten. No side effects.

But, it also means no more alcohol. Alcohol and Keppra don't mix well; together they can even cause an epileptic seizure. No more wine on the balcony. It's all about Sugar free soft drinks (remember the belly) and fresh fruit juices for me now. Non-alcoholic beers don't taste like the real thing and non-alcoholic wines are pretty much the most revolting liquids I've ever tried. They taste like foul, rotten grape juices, which in fact is exactly what they are! Don't bother trying them. They taste even worse than it sounds. No matter how expensive.

One rock on the road that I did miss was the depression. I simply didn't have one. That's my opinion anyway. I had loads of sessions with my shrink. Everyone gets a shrink and sessions are obligatory after such an ordeal. "He's not crying at all, not a hint of emotional breakdown; He's pretty good at suppressing it. Wonder what else he's suppressing, not good at all! What a poor guy."

What they didn't understand is that I'd already accepted my situation. There is no "why me?" Because there's no answer to that! Shit just happens! This time it's happened to me. Is this fair? Hell no! But what is? This may sound a little harsh, but in Geesthacht I saw people in a far worse state than me. They weren't bitchin'? No, they were coping! Why should I start moaning and whining? That only makes things worse. Everyone carries their burden. Some have big noses, some are going bald, wrong job? Not enough money? Who does? No one's responsible; no one's to blame so no furious desire for revenge. And I don't believe in karma or fate or destiny or divine intervention or whatever your preferred religion or belief may call it, but that's not a book I'm going to open now. (Maybe some time later, teaser:

Enlightenment can't be reached, we're burnin' all the time. Oh gosh, that was almost Zen!)

I've already come a long way from being comatose to wiping my own ass again. Okay! Life's harder, more complicated. The road is rocky and sometimes it's steep but when I get up to the top of the hill it'll all be downhill from there. So let's get to it. But we're doing it at my speed, got it!

So they prescribed me anti depressants.

It's a drug called a serotonin reuptake inhibitor. Serotonin is a neurotransmitter that is responsible for feeling content and complacent. It's set free at the side the synaptic gap that gets the electric impulse, crosses the gap and docks onto a receptor on the other side and says" let's all have a good time and chill a bit. Pass the word on!" And then gets absorbed. (Reuptake) so that we all don't run around with big wide grins all day and get to nothing. The inhibitor stops the absorbing part. To the effect that a whole bunch of neuro transmitters running from receptor to receptor saying: "Take it easy, everything's good." It doesn't do it to all receptors but that depends on dosage. It's very subtle and lifts your mood a touch. It also has one positive side effect. A high neurotransmitter level encourages synaptic growth. With me missing a large walnut's volume worth of brain tissue, I'll take all the neural growth I can get. No harm done in that. Lost neurons are lost forever. You're born with X of them. You die with X minus number lost on the way. Don't worry, your brain can compensate by making new connections. The brain is astoundingly flexible.

While we're talking of medication: I also take ten mg/day Baclufen, a Valium derived muscle tone reducer. 1500mg/day Keppra, my anti epileptic, which incidentally comes out of the antidepressant sector where it wasn't all too successful, but, none of the patients had epileptic seizures anymore. New package design, new name, Voila! 40mg Citalopram, my serotonin reuptake inhibitor. Plus diverse, let's call them dietary supplements, from my mum who's partner is an alternative practitioner (thanks for all the perforations Michael) supplying all the usual vitamins and minerals to exotics like, extrafrom the U.S, imported snake venomsin homeopathic dosages. They didn't harm me and who knows, maybe they helped. And if they can help, why not try them.

Traditional Chinese Medicine, like all alternative medicines has a hard standing because they're difficult to measure. Neurological disorders double so. It isn't like in "Scrubs." White blood cell count back to normal, he made it, discharge! We Neuros are victims of subjectivity. It could be better, maybe. It was better yesterday. What happened? Today it's worse. It takes lots of patience. It's a slow, arduous healing process that takes it's time. The only way to speed this up is repetition. Oh, and I get 150 to 200 units of Botox every three months.

About the Botox, I can't let it stand like that or you'll get the wrong impression of me. One unit Botox is about enough for two or three wrinkle treatments, 200 units would unwrinkle a whole box of prunes. I don't look that bad, yet. Botox has been used in the treatment of high muscle tone for decades. Botox destroys certain receptors in the synaptic gap interrupting the chemical signals that fire the muscles. This weakens the muscle tone so that the muscular counterpart gets a chance to regain strength again. This effect lasts for about four to five months until the destroyed receptors have grown back or other synaptic connections have been made to fire the muscle. With acquired high muscle tone this can mean that the new connection is used to the high fire rate and ignores it, making the muscle controllable again! That way the inward rotation of my left foot is almost completely gone. Aren't modern neurotoxins great? Let's give a hooray, for all the bacteria that had to die, for my doses.

I was scared shitless the first time, reckoning it would be worse than all the horror stories I'd read on the Internet. It was a very, very thin needle which was used to inject the Botox and at the same time functioned as an electrode. The needle was connected to an amplifier that made muscular nerve activity arable. The needle is inserted into the muscle. I could only feel the prick of the needle going through first one or two millimetres into the skin. There are no pain receptors underneath. I couldn't feel any subcutaneous action even if there were three more inches of needle to be shoved through my muscle tissue. The amplifier was switched on. A relaxed normal muscle doesn't make any noise at all. In the case of my pectoralis (It was the first one to get it. Left breast muscle) there was thunderous white noise, the nerves firing in uncontrollable chaos. Nowadays the amplifier is backed up by a sonogram which, when used together, give a very high resolution. Such a high resolution, that an experienced neurologist can even hit muscles controlling single finger joints.

It takes about a week for the Botox-effect to kick in. Thanks Doc. Nolte. I'll be back, and back, and back.

I also met lots of wonderful people. One for instance was Fred the male nurse. Wait a second; we've already had that, haven't we? What, a Fred again? Yes, but a different Fred. I started to wonder, does every clinic have a Fred? Do they have to? Do you have to pay a fine if you don't have a Fred? Is there a No-Fred-Penalty in effect? Or maybe it's the first step in a treacherous, long term plan to take over the world. First take control of the clinics, as a test. And after that, take over federal institutions. Maybe it isn't the first step and the Feds are already under Fred control and now I've uncovered their plan … My goodness! I need protection! I'm in danger. Beware of the Fred's! No, I'm not amenable to conspiracies. At least that's what the little chip in my head keeps telling me. Oh no, that was a clip… or was it? Maybe that's the reason why the last MRI Scan images I got were only in low resolution. It's a cover-up.

There were also very capable therapists especially the physio- and ergotherapists and logopaedists. I can roll my tongue again Janna (though whistling is still difficult). My arm is also moving on especially the shoulder, Udo and I are keeping the hand supple for later. I hope there are more stickers on your door Ulli. Karsten, I still hate swimming, and Anja, nobody cushioned my private parts better than you. And of course all the doctors and nurses and others, that I had the luck of being helped by. And especially nurse Juliane my secret platonic love.

Another good thing about Geesthacht was phase E. Only a handful of clinics in Germany can handle this. Let me extrapolate. Please bear with me. And a warning: boring bureaucracy stuff up ahead.

The medical system in Germany has something that is called the Barthel index. (Bx.) It's basically a catalogue of questions to determine your level of independence. X points for "can go to the toilet and clean himself", Z points for "transfer from bed to wheelchair works" and so on. The more points the more independent. To make this quite simple policy (0 points totally dependent, 100 points totally independent.) easier for the average clerk to work with, the 100 points are split up into action phases; Phase A: intensive care (Bx=0), B: early rehab/therapy, care dependent (Bx under 25) C: further rehab/therapy, some care dependent (Bx=30 to 65) D: mostly independent (Bx=70 to 100) E: after care and occupational reintegration (Bx=100+) F: Long term after-care (Bx=no idea, didn't do that.)

So Geesthacht does occupational reintegration. That's the one! Gimme that! Health insurance says no. Someone has to pay for the phase and my health insurance didn't even know that a phase E existed. I didn't want to leave the clinic at that point. I was making real progress at the time.

One moment, I'll be right back. My health insurance and pension fund deserve their own paragraphs. My affliction is hard enough to cope with as it is. But the bureaucracy involved can, and will, really drive you up the wall. My health insurance was fed up quite quickly and backed out as fast as law would let them (I think after phase C, but I can't remember for sure). No more than necessary. Not a single cent. After all they did pay a lot, months of intensive care, brain surgery twice and tons of medication. But honestly, that's what they're there for. As soon as they could, they gave my whole case to the federal pension fund. I'm still utterly and completely lost when dealing with them. And they are cleverer.

They put people over thirty in a rehab clinic of the funds choice. If in the space of a couple of weeks no tremendous improvements are made (these clinics are licenced by the pension fund so these improvements are really hard to make). This is, of course, pure speculation, (mentioned for legal reasons.) You never know who can get this book into their grubby little fingers, the "grubby" is also highly speculative and probably wrong. (See the disclaimer at the end of this book) You are then put on a pension for a trial period of three years. It may be possible that you miraculously heal without therapy and then they can send you off to work again. No further therapy necessary because as shown in the couple of weeks, it's not worth the effort. (Rehab is also more expensive than the pension, by the way.)

This is okay if you're sixty-three and standing a footstep away from your pension anyway, this makes little or no difference. If you've come this far you're probably not going to contribute all that much to the gross domestic product anymore. To say it bluntly it's not worth the effort to get you back on your feet again. If you're over sixty-five and you're already getting pension, you are not put through this procedure at all.

But I was thirty-four and needed therapy. I wanted to get back on my feet. I was in the middle of phase C. I had just applied for phase D as the summons for the pension came fluttering in, in which was stated that no more rehab was to be allotted. We filed formal protest after protest. We protested the denial of the protest, even after we weren't allowed to formally protest anymore.

In the meantime I was sent to another evaluator, this time a shrink who was to write a report on me. My wife picked me up with the car and put the wheelchair in the trunk. We found the place. Wheelchair is out of the question, steps on the way. We come into the building only to find a spiral staircase with the handrail on the wrong side. Two stories up. What kind of sadist has the idea to send a wheelchair bound handicapped person to an evaluator residing in the second story of an old house without a lift? Unless... Tactics. "He'll give up, and then we can say he never seriously wanted to have more therapy, or else why didn't he bother showing up." But they didn't reckon with me. I made it up! The pension fund knew pretty well in which state I was in. Or weren't they reading the reports? (Of course they did, anything else is highly speculative.)

Having made it up, we found his practice. He was only a shrink - he looked it too. He had wiry grey hair, was wearing an old comfortable tweed suit, the only thing missing was the red sofa. He asked his questions. Not, "how's therapy going along or how was I coping with the extreme change in your life?" But:

"How's your relationship to your mother?"

"????? ... Good."

"What's seven by thirteen?"

"Ehm ... ten by seven is seventy ... plus twenty one ..."

"How many days does a year have?"

"Solar or calendar?"

"What?"

"Solar year: 365.242 or calendar year: 366 on years evenly dividable by four, others have 365!" Gotcha!

"Ah ..., okay." And so on.

But the questions came out like a machine gun doing overtime. Not giving me time to think. After the interrogation we did the obligatory EEG. Apparently I'd passed. Phase D was approved. And guess what? I could even stay in Geesthacht. Those other clinics are probably not as bad as their reputation, for their audience, they're probably even good for the majority of their clients, but they're not good enough for me. I don't want to hold the status quo. I'm part of a small minority that's still got places to go, people to meet. I didn't want to degenerate while watching talk shows for the rest of my life.

But, anyway back to Phase E. Applied! Denied, request extend for phase D, denied, reapply for E, denied, formal complaint because of disproportionality, D extended but only four weeks, protest the denial of E ... , see what I mean? It's happening again, I'm lost. Try keeping up to that after major brain haemorrhage. Not a snowflakes chance in hell.

It seemed the pension fund was equally confused, by this time they had made so many formal errors, overstepping so many deadlines that the clinic stepped in and paid for me itself. It was going to get to it's money by court action. And I wish them the best of luck. Many thanks go to the management of the clinic for this heroic step. If you had made a business case out of it weighing up thirty years of paying out pension against another thirty years of me paying into the fund... Don't ask me. It isn't logical at all, but who said government is logical.

So I did get phase E and that works like this: On a free weekend you go and buy a notebook computer with enough power for Photoshop and Indesign. By that time my Bx was so high that I was allowed home every weekend. But I had to be back on Sunday night before the doors are closed. Then your old employer sends you material to work with. You are given some office space in the clinic and then you start working again.

At first it was slow going, especially my neglect made it difficult. I kept overseeing errors I had made on the left. But with practise I was compensating quite effectively. I still have "bad" days where errors slip by, everyone has those. The so-called puzzle pages, with lots of small product images, each with corresponding text snippets, cause the most problems. It's difficult for me to judge what's still to come and I don't leave enough whitespace to fit it in.But it's getting better from day to day. With the help of my new twelve button mouse and anew graphics tablet I was back layouting again.

Thankfully my creativity wasn't affected at all. At first it was only old material, which had already been printed. Later it was fresh "live" material, of which some was even put to paper. Best was the children's book with the name "Hasi's gone!" It's a book about the little boy named Jonas losing his beloved, stuffed rabbit. It was all about loss anxiety and overcoming this loss. How fitting. I sent my shrink a copy. The illustrations are really good and it has an "almost" happy end.

After this reintroduction to the work force based in the clinic, I was picked up by a wheelchair taxi every day from the clinic back to work. At first, two hours, then three and finally four hours, all five days of the week. Back to the same old twits. A whole bunch of new faces, while some old ones were missing. All employees are replaceable. That's life. After work, I went back to the clinic with the wheelchair taxi for lunch and my well deserved siesta.

Now the real reintegration had begun. I had a reintegration commissioner put on my case. She was there to manage the communication between Employer, clinic and me. Make sure that I could reach the coffee machine and other important questions.

Luckily I was able to go back to my former Employer. This usually isn't the case. Normally after two years of absence through sickness they find a way to sack you sooner or later. In most cases it's probably sooner. Not in my case. Thanks to TW and SM for that. I was employed the whole time. No gap in my vitae. It was like stepping back into an old used pair of shoes. It made things a lot easier.

At first I went back into my own little office but I got bored quickly and moved to the other layouters. More fun, but also more strenuous, I know, cognitive training is good for me. But I was never the gossiping type. I captivate more by hard-hitting comments from the sideline. I still find group dynamics uncanny.

You may have noticed that I have a more aggressive approach to dealing with my illness. Not all people are equipped well enough to handle that and I'm not particularly considerate or patient enough with squeamish folk. Some people get along with it quite well:

"So if you're convulsing on the floor spitting blood that isn't normal, anymore?"

5. Daily doings

So there I was, housetrained and domesticated again. Could do unbelievable tricks with my wheelchair, could even walk a short distance with my crutch. I was being successfully reintegrated in my old job. And best, stairs were no trouble anymore. Off to home. But not without several administrative hurdles being thrown in the way.

Several official requests had gone missing. Yes the pension fund again, this time collaborating with my health insurance.

And my wife and I needed a holiday first. Cruise ships are unbelievably well equipped for the handicapped. Probably has to do with their usual audience of older pensioners who have a wide range of different maladies.

If you ever get into my position, let them give you a foldable wheelchair. The advantage is that they're foldable. My wheelchair isn't. They told me that it's sturdier, it's even lighter. But believe me; you're not going to carry your wheelchair anywhere, you're going to sit on it. And if you don't weigh over 300 pounds you don't have to worry about sturdiness. Get one that's foldable! It's easier to fit through cabin doors, tight corridors on submarines, train compartments, airlocks on spaceships and other tight spaces.

Uncollapsable wheelchairs tend to be rather bulky, which is not the thing you want to have in cramped spaces. The other thing is my wheelchair needed to be one-hand driven. Because my left arm and hand are literally useless at the moment, I need to control the wheelchair with only my right, so that I don't only go in circles. My wheelchair has a second hand wheel that's smaller and drives the left wheel over an axle. The normal hand wheel is welded to the right wheel and drives it directly. To make the wheelchair smaller you have to remove the axle, then take off the wheels and for practical reasons you only do this if you have to (I think we did it once in two years). It is possible to get collapsible one-handed wheelchairs, but no one told me. Well it's too late now. My health insurance will have my head if I request a swap or even a new one, now that I can walk short distances.

But wait, my health insurance was covered by the clinic. And if I go home now and something happens, I'm not insured. We couldn't do anything else but finish my reintegration earlier. I was officially now a part of the labour force again. I was still doing four hours, which is enough for me, I am still doing four hours now and it works fine for me. Only doing half a job also meant I got half a pension. It also meant I was paying into National social insurance and also my health insurance through my employer again.

This left only one question: How am I going to get to work? No more clinics, meant no Phase E, meant no taxi anymore. Public transport was still out of the question. I don't have the capabilities needed to tackle old ladies hogging the only handicapped person seat on busses. These older women are armed with walking sticks and deafness; weapons capable of mass destruction. Sword canes fall under weapons control law; as do tasers, long swords machetes and daggers. We Germans take weapons control seriously. There are areas where you aren't even allowed to carry glass bottles. But we are allowed to drink in public if we aren't making a nuisance of ourselves.

I wasn't ready for that war, yet. But one day, I'm going to beat your handicapped IDs with twenty percent hearing loss, with my one hundred percent extreme mobility impaired ID and blow you out of that seat. But for now you're safe, because the pensions fund is paying my taxi to and from work. Now you're probably thinking: "How did he get that? " Well it was quite easy. It's always cleverer to pick an opponent you know, it's strategically more effective. You've already got a feel for the enemy from previous encounters. Old folks are so unpredictable, even erratic. Not so the pensions fund.

So we took up the fight with the pension fund again. Request for help with the taxi costs was sent. The answer came with a request for a report from my neurologist. This was to be expected, nothing new for us and not for my neurologist either, who wrote reports on an almost weekly basis for me at the time. Several days later the denial came. But the neurological report was still on my kitchen table. Nobody could have read or even evaluated it. We hadn't even sent it. This was new. It was a totally different approach from the Pension fund. How refreshing. It was quite unexpected, almost refreshing, but very easy to get on to. They were trying to intimidate us. But to no avail. We officially protested the denial and waited.

After several weeks of waiting and several hours of trying to phone up the, for me, responsible contact person, we then tried twiddling with the direct-call digits [long number in Berlin]-321 instead of [long number in Berlin]-322. After a short number of failures we finally got a woman on the line that wasn't permanently out to lunch. After explaining my case my wife asked if she could help us with the taxi costs as we had requested. "No can do, I'm sorry, but I can get you a full time personal assistant who can help getting paper for the printer or get me some coffee if I so wished."

My wife almost throttled her through the telephone. Believe me, she can. Every small walk even to the coffee machine is therapy for me; an assistant would make things worse. Instead, regaining her wits she cleverly asked the woman: "If we give that up, will that help with the taxi costs?" It seems that someone at the fund could calculate that it was cheaper giving me a taxi flat rate rather than a full time personal assistant, although I wouldn't have minded a young brunette (I'm not for blondes, I've got enough of those in the family,) at my disposal. And from there it all went quickly. They approved it for a year. It beats paying yourself by a long shot.

But I can understand why my wife is traumatised every time official mail comes by. That's because it's been mostly denials or fund cuts or other bad news the last couple of years. I did get good news once. My pension was raised, by unbelievable 20 cents/month, which means I can buy myself an ice cream more, but only once a year of course.

The only ones that reacted well were the guys from my private occupational disability insurance. "At least it's a clear case." That was the only comment from them. A little inappropriate, but they were right. They've got a lot to do with subjective maladies like burnouts and depression. In my case there was a clear organic reason for my occupational disability. They sent my wife an inch thick pamphlet of forms to fill out and we only heard from them when they need an update, which is every three years. And they pay nicely. You've never heard of that insurance before? Then get up and inform yourself. Now! They're saving my ass right now.

Somehow everything I do has become therapy. Even going to the toilet, nowadays free-handed, is work for me. More weight on the left leg. Try to bend the knee, rotate the pelvis a lot more to the right and tip it a little to the front.

Keep full weight on left leg while right leg swings through. Shift weight to the right, bend the left knee again swing the left leg through, don't forget the pelvis, and pull the foot up, land on the heel. Roll over the whole length of the foot, knees bent! Start over.

Not all too long ago I tried to walk home from therapy. It's not too far, just a kilometre and I would have made it if it hadn't started to snow at half distance. The cold upped my stress level and the resulting muscle tone did the rest to slow me to a stop. I had to phone my wife out of a meeting for her to pick me up, all that only several hundred meters from home. Some weather god from above had said "No, not yet!"

Sitting, torso straight in all three planes, stretch the left side, tip the pelvis to the front, chest out without your back being hollow. Listening to more than two people at the same time is still challenging. Whilst talking, no mumbling, watch your articulation, look at the person you're speaking to, filter out background noise while you're listening.

Try the following: The next time you have a conversation, try to think of something completely else. Like your big right toe. Can you feel the sock between skin and shoe? Is the nail too long again? Move it to the left, the right, up, then down, twiddle it, rub it against the toe next to it. Try to grab your sock with both of them. Have an interesting conversation?

Whilst writing this book I constantly have to look at the beginning of each and every line over and over again to not miss a spelling, punctuation or grammar mistake on the left side. And believe me there were a lot! And it feels so wrong! The normal direction while reading is left to right. I have to go from right to left consciously.

Not every thing has to happen at a conscious level. Even in my case routine sets in at some point. But it is astonishing how complicated, easy, everyday actions become when you are forced to think about them. Every new action opens a whole catalogue of questions that spool through my brain: Can I do it? Can I do it with aid, who is close enough to help? Do I have to bend my leg or will it work without? Do I have to use left hand? Can my teeth help? Should I stand up or can do it sitting? Is it even worth the effort? I get used to it, train, train, train. Do it again. And again. Each time it'll get a little bit better/faster/easier/further. Sometimes so little, that you can't see the improvement at all.

So I keep trying even if it doesn't work first time round. So what! It never does. No one said this was going to be easy! I've got nothing to lose and all to win. And don't forget there are some things I can't do. If I fall, I can't get up. I have to swallow my pride and ask for help. Most people are glad to help. It pushes their self-esteem. "See, I'm one of the good guys that help people in need!" And they're right. If you ask nicely they will. A "Please" at the right moment will go a long way. Very important are clear instructions. Most people are afraid that they'll do something wrong. If you're in a situation you've never encountered yourself, say so. "I have no ideas on how you're going to put me back on my feet but we'll do it together!" I have more difficulties telling people I don't want help. I've thought of a creative answer to: "can I help? "I say "yes, I need to borrow your time machine!" The why is easily explained. It breaks the ice nicely". There are people who have too much self-esteem or too little time to help. But to tell you the truth, they have a bigger problem than I do and they're mostly help resistant. So I don't worry much about this minority.

One other thing, people in wheelchairs never do wrong. Believe me; you roll into someone's ankles. Not on purpose, but it happens, sometimes hard enough to cause a bruise. Whoever gets hit turns around with a face ready to explode in anger. It switches quickly to first astonishment, then pity, then embarrassment. All in a very short time or, all at the same time, this can be quite funny. And here comes the strange part. Out of the mouth that only seconds ago would have ripped out your vital organs comes a quiet "Sorry, are you okay?" "No, I think my wheelchair's been mortally wounded and I'm not sure if it's going to make it, you twit!" I've put serious thought into rotating razor blades, spikes or a chainsaw at full throttle across the front of my wheelchair. Just to give people something to think about. The nerve of some people!

Let's try another experiment. Stand up and try the following: stretch your stronger arm out at right angles to your torso. Imagine there's a bottle of your favourite drink just out of reach try to grab the neck of the bottle. You're really thirsty, try harder. Stretch! ... Now hold it! Bend your arm at the elbow just a little giving your biceps some room. Now let your triceps pull your arm straight again.

Pull against the Biceps. Let them see-saw, building up the pressure. Now make a fist, keep up the pressure in your arm. Make the fist hard as a rock. You're not going hard enough; your knuckles aren't white yet. And now, hold it! Just for a minute, that's only sixty seconds, you can do it! Right angles, I said! ...Hold it! ... Three ... two, one! You're done! Pretty exhausting isn't it. I've been doing that all day, bar sleep, for close to three years now. And not only with my arm but also left leg, left side of my torso, neck, hip. I think you understand me a little better now and why I need my siesta.

Marathons are for wussies! Oh, how comfortable was life in the nicely padded world of the clinic. But I prefer cold, hard reality anytime. You grow along with your tasks. We Neuros grow twice so. Things are getting better, my left knee is starting to bend actively. I've been upgraded to a Nordic walking stick. I've left the crutch standing in a corner. My second stick was an ebony cane with massive sterling silver handle called "Old Fritz" named after the last German emperor who had one of the same design. It was forbidden by my therapists; I tended to hang myself into it, putting too much weight in my right arm. You can't do that with a Nordic walking stick. It makes me more upright.

But it is more exhausting. I think that these physio- and ergo-terrorists have fun in coming up with harder, more exhausting and more tiring things for me to do. Just when you're getting into the hang of things; Okay, that's enough, off to the next level. I think they're just modern torturers in disguise.

They all have a adisticstrain. This "we're only helping" thing is just a cheap façade to pick up girls. I know, I know, we all come of our own free will. And you're right.

Sometimes this newly acquired stability and mobility can lead to carelessness and wanton actions, I topple over: I closed the door of my taxi with a little too much verve, did an ungraceful pirouette and crumpled to the floor legs intertwined. I fractured my left Metacarpal IV (bone in the base joint and hand of the ring finger, left hand.) Also known as the boxer or idiots fracture.

But it is getting better I catch myself before falling in over ninety percent of my wobblers. Three Ergo sessions and two physio sessions a week do their job nicely. And as the saying goes: you can't make an omelette without breaking eggs, and sometimes you break fingers. The positive effects outweigh the negative in the long run.

I also do forty-five minutes of Hippotherapy at weekends on our beloved but somewhat gluttonous Icelandic horse Kolskœr. But only if it's not raining or snowing. Yes, I admit, I'm a sunshine rider. Well I don't actually ride. I just sit on the horse, which is then led, I don't influence the direction or speed at all. Even if by pure definition riding is: "a form of transportation on the back of an animal".

Sometimes I try to change directions by shifting weight and applying pressure with my inner thighs. Sometimes I think it even works. Especially if there's a fence coming and the horse has to change direction anyway, but just sitting on it is hard enough anyway. It's an incredible workout for the whole torso. My whole body swings from side to side, up and down, front to back. The horse is swaying this way and that, constantly in motion. My muscles have to do overtime just to keep me in balance.

The first time lasted only fifteen minutes and I just barely survived the ordeal. By now I can go a good half hour without breaking into a sweat. Our horse gives up before me. My wife an experienced equestrian (she was eight the first time on a horse without notable pause) keeps asking me if I enjoy it at all. The truth is no, not really. Don't get me wrong, I like being with animals, and the farm feeling, that's all really nice. But sitting on a horse is hard work and unfortunately that's what it is. Work. I can't wait for it to become recreation, and my first ride with my wife into the nearby forest.

You're probably thinking: "how the hell does he get up on a horse, he can barely walk and then he tries to ride? Horses are big animals." For one the Icelandic horses are smaller, more compact than these overbred big horses and are, for their size, more powerful and better built for weight carrying. They are, simply put: Sturdier. They are also hardier and they don't need boxes over winter. They just grow longer hair and stand in the falling snow. Secondly the stable owners built a ramp just for me so that I can climb up. Thanks a lot for that.

My left hand is my only real worry at the moment. But if I've got one thing it's time. Its time will come. A neurologist who probably stuck his head a bit too far out of the window told me than seventy percent can be regained in ten years time. So I've got plenty of time to do work on it. I'm pretty sure I'm not going to be able play the piano but I couldn't beforehand either, so who gives. I've bought a cornet, a smaller trumpet, which I can play with one hand, but as I said, I'm a lazy slob, and regular practicing was never one of my strengths. So I would rather listen to one of my over a thousand jazz CDs. I'm looking into the young Scandinavians at the moment. But they're a little too precise, electronic and too "ambient" for my taste. I prefer hard bop like Horace Silver, Stanley Turrentine and Joe Pass. Miles Davis is okay, but Louis Armstrong has loads more "feel" in his play.

I've developed a hat-quirk. I would never ever have even worn hats before. Maybe I'm just getting old and eccentric. Interestingly also, that in the clinics I'd lost my taste for wieners. This was very disturbing. But thankfully I've overcome that weird phobia and wieners are back on my diet. Coffee too, I never liked it much and one cup always brought me to the brink of agitated. At first I thought it was a counteragent to the side effects of my Baclufen, it's now a regular. I never leave the house without my "double espresso grande". We even bought a fully automated coffee machine. Believe me it's needed as much as the dishwasher.

I always say I've been decelerated and I can go with that. You get to see a lot more of the quite decent scenery if you take your time and don't rush through life. You start to notice the details. Besides my Grandfather always said "all'ns het s'in tied"(everything has its own time). And He was always right.

What many people don't understand is that a part of me really did die in that night. But that's okay. The rest of my brain is pretty good at compensating and a lot of what I lost was what I lost most was innocence. And I'm not going to miss that much. I've had a major change of perspective. All the little worries people have seem so indignificant in the larger picture. Well, Let's see what else I can salvage in time. Until then you're going to have to put up with a new better, brighter Tim with a whole bucket of new experiences to go with. I may be a little more morbid but I think I'm allowed to be after several near death experiences. But like I said at the beginning: I'm doing fine.

So here I am; half of my brain damaged, left half paralysed, left side only half a feeling. About half my estimated life expectancy is gone. I have half a job, I'm half a pensioner. But the glass is half full and not half empty! If someday I should put this story to paper I'm going to call it "Half Time." Because that's where I am at the moment and when the game goes on, I'm going to storm out of the locker room with loads of fresh energy and I'm going to win this game, even if it's the last thing I do!

Thanks to:

Wellhausen & Marquardt Medien, Physiosport HanSa. Ergoteam Ottensen, MPM GmbH, HELIOS Klinik Geesthacht, Schön Klinik Hamburg Eilbek, Universitäts Klinikum Hamburg Eppendorf and all their employees. And most of all, my thanks to all those I forgot to mention. Sorry about that. It won't happen again.

Disclaimer:

Everything occurring in this text, technical and medical descriptions, ideas, and opinions are highly assumptive and speculative and come from a totally deranged and heavily brain damaged mind and should not be taken too seriously and definitely not literally!